ZEBRAS

LIVING WILD

Published by Creative Education
P.O. Box 227, Mankato, Minnesota 56002
Creative Education is an imprint of The Creative Company
www.thecreativecompany.us

Design and production by Mary Herrmann
Art direction by Rita Marshall
Printed in the United States of America

Photographs by Alamy (Claudia Adams, AF archive, Martin Harvey, Moviestore collection Ltd, North Wind Picture Archives, Antonio Pagano), Dreamstime (Steve Allen, Anky10, Marina Cano, Fernando Cerecedo, Neal Cooper, Designpicssub, Steffen Foerster, Hedrus, Holger Karius, Holly Kuchera, Roman Murushkin, Duncan Noakes, Cobus Olivier, Orxystock, Perseomedusa, Nico Smit, Mogens Trolle, Enna Van Duinen), Getty Images (Annie Griffiths Belt, DEA PICTURE LIBRARY, Richard du Toit, Suzi Eszterhas, Bobby Haas, Martin Harvey, Lanz von Horsten, Frank Krahmer, Art Wolfe), iStockphoto (Carsten Brandt, Jose Gil, Mogens Trolle)

Library of Congress Cataloging-in-Publication Data
Gish, Melissa.
Zebras / by Melissa Gish.
p. cm. — (Living wild)
Includes bibliographical references and index.
Summary: A look at zebras, including their habitats, physical characteristics such as their striped fur, behaviors, relationships with humans, and protected status in the world today.
ISBN 978-1-60818-173-5
1. Zebras—Juvenile literature. I. Title.

QL737.U62G57 2012
599.665'7—dc23   2011035797

First Edition
9 8 7 6 5 4 3 2 1

CREATIVE EDUCATION

ZEBRAS

Melissa Gish

A herd of more than 100 zebras approaches the river
after a long trek across the salt-desert landscape.

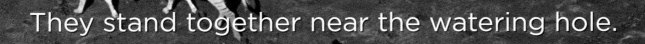

They stand together near the watering hole.

It is mid–August, the height of summer in Botswana's Makgadikgadi (*muh-KAH-dee-KAH-dee*) Pans Game Reserve, and the Boteti River has dried up, leaving only scattered pools of water. A herd of more than 100 zebras approaches the river after a long trek across the salt-desert landscape. They stand together near the watering hole. Some bend their necks and munch on dry grass. Others quietly snort and whinny at each other, signaling contentment at having reached the water source. Other animals are drinking there already, including wildebeest, Thomson's gazelles, and lions. The zebras move cautiously toward the water, keeping their eyes on the lions. As the zebras drink, a wave rises nearby and laps against the shore. Sensing danger, the zebras suddenly explode backward just as a crocodile bursts from the water and lunges onto the muddy shore. The zebras were lucky—this time.

WHERE IN THE WORLD THEY LIVE

■ **Plains Zebra**
from Ethiopia
to South Africa

■ **Mountain Zebra**
Namibia, South
Africa

■ **Grevy's Zebra**
northern Kenya,
Ethiopia

The three zebra species are native to the African continent alone. The five living subspecies of plains zebra are found in eastern and southern Africa, from Ethiopia to South Africa, while the two subspecies of mountain zebra are restricted to parts of Namibia and South Africa. The single specimen of Grevy's zebra lives in Kenya and Ethiopia. Colored squares indicate the species' common locations.

HORSES OF AFRICA

Zebras belong to the genus *Equus* (*EE-kwis*), which means "horse" in Latin and includes the **domesticated** horses and three species of wild ass. Members of this genus are called equids and include a number of subspecies, or breeds, characterized by their straight cutting teeth, long necks and heads, and powerful legs, each with a single toe covered by a tough hoof. The three species of zebra—Grevy's, mountain, and plains (also known as common)—are the only equids found exclusively in Africa. Once widespread across Central Africa, Grevy's zebras now inhabit only northern Kenya and scattered areas of Ethiopia. These zebras have **adapted** to living in dry, semi-desert habitats. Mountain zebras, able to run on uneven ground, live on the rocky slopes of Namibia's and South Africa's various mountain ranges. Plains zebras, the most abundant species, are found from Ethiopia to South Africa, with most living on the grasslands of Kenya and Tanzania.

Zebras can be further divided into subspecies based on size, stripe pattern, and other characteristics. There are six subspecies of plains zebra: Burchell's, Chapman's, Crawshay's, Grant's, and Selous's zebras, as well as the

Hipparion was an early horse that lived in Africa and elsewhere from 23 million to about 780,000 years ago.

Zebras are ungulates, or hoofed mammals, just like llamas, rhinoceroses, moose, sheep, and camels.

A zebra has seven cervical vertebrae, or neck bones, which is the same number that humans have.

quagga, which was hunted to **extinction** in the 19th century. The two kinds of mountain zebra are the Cape and Hartmann's zebras. The Grevy's zebra is the only one of its kind and is currently categorized by the International Union for Conservation of Nature (IUCN) as endangered. Most zebras, except the quagga and Cape mountain zebra, were named for the naturalists or explorers who discovered them. The Grevy's zebra was named for Jules Grévy, president of France from 1879 to 1887, who received one as a gift from the emperor of what is now Ethiopia. The word "zebra" comes from Congolese, the native language of the inhabitants of the Congo River region of Central Africa.

Zebras are mammals. All mammals produce milk to feed their young and, with the exceptions of the egg-laying platypuses and hedgehog-like echidnas of Australia, give birth to live offspring. Mammals are also warm-blooded. This means that their bodies try to maintain a healthy, constant temperature that is usually warmer than their surroundings. Zebras live in hot climates and cool themselves by sweating—just like humans. The sweat **evaporates** to cool the blood just beneath the skin. Zebras sometimes also pant like dogs, which reduces their internal body temperature.

Young male zebras may avoid fights with older males by nuzzling them, an action that demonstrates submission.

Zebras breed remarkably well in captivity, and foals are born in zoos around the world every year.

Adult male zebras are called stallions, and females are called mares. Baby zebras are called foals. Standing more than 5 feet (1.5 m) tall at the shoulder and stretching 11.5 feet (3.5 m) from the tip of its nose to the end of its 30-inch (76 cm) tail, the Grevy's zebra is not only the largest zebra, but it is also the largest of all wild equids. An adult male can weigh nearly 1,000 pounds (453.5 kg). The other zebra species and subspecies range in size smaller than the Grevy's, but the smallest is the Cape mountain zebra, at only 4 feet (1.2 m) tall and 7 feet (2.1 m) long, not counting its 15-inch (38 cm) tail. The average weight among all plains zebra subspecies is 700 pounds (318 kg).

The zebra's striped fur, called a coat, is short; a striped mane of stiff, bristly hairs runs down the back of the neck, and the tail ends in a tuft of coarse hair. Every zebra has a different stripe pattern, and the type of stripe pattern varies among species and subspecies. For example, the plains zebras have wide, creamy-white stripes, but Grevy's zebras have narrow, bright-white stripes. Chapman's and Selous's zebras have brownish stripes, called shadow stripes, between the black-and-white stripes. Some zebras' stripes run all the way down their legs to their hooves, but others have stripes

Zebra foals are born white with brown stripes, and their manes temporarily cover their entire back down to their tails.

Because grass and leaves are neither very filling nor energizing, zebras must eat continuously all day long.

that cover only the body, leaving the legs white, as is the case with Burchell's zebras. **Zoologists** generally agree that zebras have white coats with dark stripes; however, the skin **pigment** under the white coat is black.

Zebras have velvety fur on their muzzles, and long hairs in their ears and long eyelashes protect against blowing dirt and dust. All zebras are herbivores, meaning they eat only vegetation. About 90 percent of a zebra's diet is grass, but shrubs and the leaves of small trees provide food as well. A zebra's front teeth, called incisors, are designed for clipping grass close to the ground. The back teeth, called molars, are sharply ridged for grinding food into a pulp. Zebras have four pairs of molars in each jaw. Constant chewing causes the molars to wear down, so a zebra's teeth keep growing throughout its life.

Zebras need water nearly every day. They gather at lakesides and watering holes with other animals to drink, ever on the lookout for predators. Zebras have an excellent sense of smell and keen hearing. They can pivot their ears to detect sounds from all directions. And with their eyes set wide apart and high on their heads, zebras can see almost all the way around them without turning their heads. But

Zebras show their teeth while vocalizing, braying deeply to indicate territory and locate mates from a distance.

Plains zebras have about 52 stripes on their coats, mountain zebras have about 110 stripes, and Grevy's zebras have about 160 stripes.

As a zebra grazes, ticks congregate on its body, supplying oxpeckers with a feast.

when its head is down at the water's edge for a drink, a zebra is vulnerable. Stepping too near what it believes to be a harmless, muddy log, a zebra could find its head suddenly seized by a crocodile rushing from the water.

Zebras can swim but prefer to avoid it whenever possible. During certain times of the year, zebras and other animals struggle to cross swollen rivers in search of food. Zebras sometimes drown during these endeavors. To escape predators on land, zebras can run 40 miles (64 km) per hour. Lions can match this speed but only for about 100 yards (91 m). If struck from behind, a zebra will kick its attacker. One blow from a zebra's powerful hind legs can shatter the bones of a lion.

Zebras have a special relationship with the oxpecker, a bird that shares their grassy habitats. Also known as the tickbird, the oxpecker is a grayish-brown bird that is slightly smaller than a robin. One species has a red beak, and the other has a yellow beak. These birds provide the zebra with a cleaning service by eating **parasites** off the animals' hides. They also eat tiny insects that invade wounds in animal flesh, which helps speed the healing process.

Zebras can easily run through the shallow water of a low-lying marsh, especially if a predator is in pursuit.

Zebras find safety in numbers and maintain a vigilant lookout for predators throughout the day and night.

ALL TOGETHER NOW

Zebras are social animals that live in groups called bands, harems, or herds. During certain times of year, bands and harems may join together to form herds of up to 200 zebras. In all species, some bands consist of all females and their immature offspring, while others, called bachelor bands, consist of all young males. There is no leadership in most bands, and many members come and go, joining different bands throughout the year. Plains and mountain zebra bands are nomadic, which means they travel freely from place to place. Grevy's zebra bands are territorial, living in established areas near water sources, and a dominant stallion will defend his band's territory, which can be up to five square miles (13 sq km) in size, from rivals seeking leadership status.

Zebras form harems during mating season. A stallion may gather a group of 2 to 5 mares and his offspring with these mares into a harem consisting of up to 15 zebras. The stallion will mate only with members of his harem, and he will prevent other males from approaching them. Young stallions build their harems by invading existing harems and stealing young females called fillies.

If a member of a zebra band is injured in an attack, the other zebras will surround it and try to protect it from further harm.

The Cape mountain zebra has reddish markings on its nose that help distinguish it from other species and subspecies.

Scientists fear that habitat shifts may cause Cape and Hartmann's mountain zebras to interbreed, leading to the extinction of purebred subspecies.

Stallions defend their harems from rival stallions, protect young and weak members from predators such as lions and cheetahs, and lead their followers to food and water sources. Sometimes dozens of zebra bands and harems travel together, forming massive herds that provide individuals with a form of **camouflage** called disruptive coloration. When zebras stand in a group, their stripes appear to blend together, making it difficult for predators to pick out individuals. Thus, predators have learned to be patient with zebras, hiding and waiting for the animals to let down their guard.

While their bands or harems graze, stallions remain watchful. When a stallion senses danger, he stands still and arches his neck, listening and looking. The other zebras immediately recognize this cautionary behavior and stop grazing. Sometimes, as when a group of lions moves to a shady spot simply to sleep, the threat passes. To be safe, though, the zebras wrangle their foals into the center of the herd to protect them and then stand in a semicircle facing the threat. They continue grazing but keep their eyes on the invader.

Other times, the threat is imminent, and the stallion will bark a warning. All the zebras will stomp and snort.

Rival stallions aggressively defend their territories, and a dominant male will not give up a filly without a fight.

Lions are not fast runners over long distances, so they hunt cooperatively and rely on the element of surprise.

Mothers may bark and yip at their young. When a lion or cheetah rushes out from tall grass, the zebras run, yipping and snorting. They stay close together, protecting the foals. Unfortunately for the zebras, their attackers often win, bringing down members that get separated from the herd.

Adults will not necessarily die for their offspring. It is better for a mother to let her foal fall prey than for her to die. She must remain alive to continue reproducing, instinctively fulfilling her role in the African **ecosystem**. This is important not only for zebras but also for the many animals that rely on the zebra as a food source. Big cats eat the organs and strip meat from the bones. Then vultures pick the remnants of flesh from the bones, and hyenas follow by eating the bones. Nothing goes to waste.

Zebras that survive African predators to reach old age may live 25 years. In captivity, zebras can live about 30 years. Some studies have suggested that wild zebras live only about nine years on average before falling prey to predators. Mares are ready to mate when they are about three years old, and stallions begin to mate after age four. Several stallions will approach a harem containing a filly in estrus, which is a period during which a female animal gives off a scent signaling that she is ready to mate. During the filly's two- to four-week estrus, her father will fend off many of these rivals, but eventually, the battles wear him down. After the filly is driven out of the harem, she becomes the subject of fights among the rival stallions, who kick and bite each other until one emerges as the winner.

A filly may be stolen several times before she mates and gives birth. She will then usually remain with the father of her foal and continue to mate with him for her entire life. Mating seasons vary, depending on the species. The **gestation** period for zebras is 12 to 13 months. Grevy's

Zebras use their front teeth and lips to nibble on the necks and backs of their band members, a behavior that strengthens family bonds.

Except for foals, which sleep lying down, zebras sleep standing up, and one zebra always stands guard when the others rest.

zebras are usually born between July and November. Cape mountain zebras are typically born between December and February, while Hartmann's mountain zebra foals may arrive as late as April. All subspecies of plains zebra give birth between October and March.

Mares give birth to a single foal while lying on their sides. At birth, mountain zebra foals are the smallest, weighing about 55 pounds (25 kg). Newborn plains zebra foals weigh about 70 pounds (32 kg), and Grevy's zebra foals can weigh up to 88 pounds (40 kg). All zebra foals are able to stand within 20 minutes of birth and can run within 2 hours. For the first few days of its life, the foal is separated from the other members of its band because it must learn to recognize its mother's stripe pattern, voice, and scent. This behavior is called imprinting, and it will enable the foal to always find its mother—especially in the flurry of a stampede to evade predators.

Although foals begin eating grass at about 1 week of age, they rely on their mother's milk for nourishment for the first 7 to 10 months of their lives. Despite being nearly full-grown by this age, the young zebras may remain with their mothers for up to two more years—until the

males leave to join other bands or the females are stolen
and forced into neighboring harems. The mother will be
ready to mate again when her previous offspring is about
three years old.

Zebra reproduction is tied to the climate in which the
animals live. During times of drought, when vegetation
is scarce, mares will not usually mate successfully or
produce viable offspring. In times of sufficient rainfall,
when grass is plentiful, mares are healthier and can
reproduce abundantly.

*Some zebras "bathe" in areas called
dust bowls to stretch their muscles
and ease itching from insect bites.*

SEEING STRIPES

Zebras have been part of African storytelling since the dawn of human communication. Their unique stripes make them perfect subjects for pourquoi stories. The word "pourquoi" is French for the question "why?" Pourquoi are tales that explain why something in nature is the way it is. In the case of zebras, there are many pourquoi that tell how zebras got their stripes.

One story from Namibia explains that it started with a zebra and a baboon getting in a fight over a watering hole. The zebra kicked the baboon, sending it skidding across some rocks, but then tripped over the baboon's campfire. The story provides reasons why the baboon's rump, which was scraped on the rocks, is now bare and bright red, and why the zebra, which landed on burning sticks in the campfire, now has black stripes across its body.

Another tale from South Africa explains that none of the animals on Earth had color when they were first created. One day, the Creator invited all the animals to come to his cave to select their coats. Leopards, lions, ostriches, warthogs, flamingos, and all the other animals

When chased, a zebra will run in a zigzag pattern, making it difficult for the attacker to keep its eyes on the zebra.

The zebra is one of many exotic animals featured in costumes for London's annual Notting Hill Carnival.

of South Africa came to the cave. The zebra, however, lingered on the plains, stuffing himself with grass. When his belly had grown enormous, the zebra finally stopped eating and went to the cave. The zebra was too late, though. The other animals had picked all the finest coats, and there was nothing left but a small black coat. The zebra put on the coat, but it was too tight. The Creator laughed and told the zebra this was his punishment for not coming promptly when he was summoned. The zebra pulled the coat around his swollen belly and held his breath to button it. But as soon as he let out his breath, the coat ripped in a dozen places, leaving him covered with tattered black strips. And that is why, South Africans say, the zebra wears a coat of black stripes.

Because of that unique coat, many African cultures honor the zebra as a symbol of beauty and speed, and certain ethnic groups have adopted the striking appearance of the zebra in their costumes. In Uganda, the Karamojong people paint stripes on their faces and use the zebra's tail as an integral part of the traditional **regalia** worn in ceremonies and dances. The Dan people of Ivory Coast in western Africa—where zebras were once

abundant—carved zebra masks from wood and wore them during hunting celebrations to symbolize their desire for speed. Today, people from Ghana to the Democratic Republic of the Congo continue to wear zebra masks to ward off evil spirits or to celebrate festivals.

Zebras are considered a sacred animal to the Dube people of KwaZulu-Natal, South Africa, and the hunting of zebras—as well as neighboring wildebeest and their natural

During festive dances, native Zulu dancers may wear traditional zebra masks to summon the spirits of their ancestors.

It took many failed attempts at domestication before Europeans realized that zebras were better off in the wild.

predators, lions—has long been strictly regulated by location and season. The name "Dube" means "zebra" in the tribe's language, and the zebra is regarded as the tribe's **totem** animal. Killing a zebra out of season or leaving a zebra carcass unused after a hunt is believed to trigger bad luck.

In Botswana, the zebra is valued as an important wilderness resource. Two zebras appear prominently on the nation's **coat of arms**, holding up a shield emblazoned with images representing industry, natural resources, and agriculture—all vital to the economic health of Botswana. Also, the nation's soccer team is nicknamed the Zebras and features a pair of zebras on its logo.

A multicolored zebra named Yipes is pictured on the logo for Fruit Stripe Gum, which has remained popular since it was invented in the 1960s. A successful zebra

conservation strategy was put forth in 1996 by then owner Hershey Foods Corporation when it donated five cents from every jumbo-size pack of Fruit Stripe Gum sold to the World Wildlife Fund (WWF). More than $100,000 was contributed in this way to the WWF's wildlife preservation efforts.

An overly self-confident, loud-mouthed zebra gained popularity among moviegoers in 2005 when DreamWorks SKG released the animated film *Madagascar*. An unlikely group of friends living in New York's Central Park Zoo—Marty the zebra (voiced by Chris Rock), Alex the lion, Melman the giraffe, and Gloria the hippopotamus—decide to leave their cages in search of wide-open spaces. They end up on the island of Madagascar, and their adventures ultimately led to a

A crew of eight animal trainers and wranglers was needed to corral the zebras in the movie *Racing Stripes*.

film sequel, *Madagascar: Escape 2 Africa*, in 2008. In this second film, Marty meets his relatives during a great **migration** and learns more than he ever wanted to know about the mystery of zebra stripes.

A real-life zebra with a horselike personality became the only captive zebra ever to star in a North American traveling rodeo. The zebra, named Ribbons, was purchased by wrangler and rodeo performer Tom White of Carlsbad, New Mexico, in the early 1950s. White trained Ribbons to jump, race, and perform other tricks. The pair performed at rodeos around the United States for more than a decade. Ribbons was then purchased by the owners of Old Tucson, a movie studio in Arizona, where many western movies have been made and tours are conducted. Ribbons lived and performed at the studio until he died in 1969.

More recently, zebra actors were featured in the 2005 Warner Bros. film *Racing Stripes*, in which an orphaned zebra named Stripes grows up believing he has the makings of a racehorse. His new owner, a girl named Channing, has faith in the abandoned zebra and helps him achieve his dreams. In reality, zebras typically do not make good racehorses, rodeo horses, circus performers, or even cart

pullers, yet people have tried for more than 2,000 years to train zebras for these purposes. Beginning in ancient Rome, zebras were made to perform in circuses, and for hundreds of years people tried to domesticate them— almost always without success. **Captive-reared** zebras can be trained to be tame and perform simple behaviors for movies such as *Racing Stripes*, which utilized eight zebras, each taught to perform a specific behavior. However, since zebras have a natural fear of humans, and their wide body shape is not well suited to wearing a saddle, people have generally given up on trying to force them into the same roles as domesticated horses.

Just like zebras in real life, no two animated zebras in Madagascar: Escape 2 Africa *have exactly the same stripe pattern.*

The first Hyracotherium fossil was discovered in England in 1841, and later specimens were nicknamed "dawn horses."

SURVIVAL IN A CHANGING WORLD

The oldest-known zebra ancestor—what scientists consider to have been the first horse—was no larger than a cocker spaniel and weighed about 40 pounds (18 kg). *Hyracotherium* emerged about 50 million years ago and lived throughout North America, Europe, and Asia. Its body and head were shaped like a horse's, and it also had small teeth and hoofed toes on its padded feet—four on each front foot and three on each back foot. *Hyracotherium* existed for about 15 million years before being replaced by animals better equipped to eat the changing vegetation. As plants became woodier and grasses more fibrous, herbivores such as horses **evolved** to feature grinding teeth.

The prehistoric horses gradually grew larger. *Parahippus*, which existed about 20 million years ago, was the size of a German shepherd. The extra toes of the early horses then began to disappear, as evidenced in 12-million-year-old fossils of *Pliohippus*, which had only stubs on each side of its center hoof. Many early horses thrived in North America until about 10,000 to 8,000 years ago. A mysterious mass extinction took place then,

Zebras like to roll in mud, which attaches to insect pests and loose fur; later, the zebra shakes the dried mud off to clean itself.

wiping out many species of mammals and birds in North America. Wild horses and asses continued to evolve in Europe and Asia, and in Africa their relatives became the zebras we know today.

Grevy's zebras once numbered in the millions, but in the 19th and early 20th centuries, relentless overhunting led to their drastic decline. In recent decades, as cities and farms spread into zebra territories, habitat loss and fragmentation have introduced greater threats to zebra survival. As a result of competition with domestic grazing animals, fences that block zebras from reaching water sources, and other human interference, only about 2,500 Grevy's zebras now exist in the wild.

Conservationists are desperate to find ways to protect the remaining Grevy's zebras and increase their population. Paul Muoria is a Kenyan wildlife biologist leading a study of Grevy's zebras for the African Wildlife Foundation in Kenya. Since 2002, Muoria's project has counted and tracked zebra populations and monitored human interactions with zebras. His team also has a say in government and community efforts to prevent the **poaching** of zebras.

In 2010, Muoria's team fitted five zebras with electronic collars designed to gather data on zebra movement and land use. Each collar contained a **Global Positioning System** (GPS) device that would record the animal's position as it moved. The zebras were shot with a tranquilizer dart, fitted with a collar, and then released. Muoria's team hoped the data they gathered would help them develop conservation strategies allowing for the coexistence of zebras and humans.

The Cape mountain zebra shares the Grevy's endangered status on the IUCN Red List of Threatened Species. Despite the establishment of Mountain Zebra National Park in South Africa in 1937, overhunting continued to devastate Cape mountain zebra populations. By the 1950s, fewer than 100 individuals existed. Further conservation efforts, including the establishment of more protected wildlife areas such as Karoo National Park in 1979, helped the Cape mountain zebra population bounce back, and it now stands at roughly 1,200. The number is still far too low to relieve this zebra of its endangered status, though.

A major strategy for rebuilding zebra populations involves relocating the animals to various protected

Radio collars are prime tools for the Grevy's Zebra Trust, which focuses on zebra conservation in Ethiopia and Kenya.

Believed to have gone extinct in 1910, Burchell's zebras survived and were recognized as existing again in 2004.

Zebras usually graze no more than 20 miles (32 km) from a water source and cannot go more than 4 or 5 days without water.

places in order to broaden the **genetic** makeup of those areas, and private citizens are often enlisted in these efforts. For example, the Bushmans Kloof Wilderness Reserve near Cape Town, South Africa, is a private preserve and home to 30 Cape mountain zebras—the largest private collection of these zebras in the world. Protected from predators, the zebras, as well as springbok, eland, and other hoofed animals, are allowed to flourish in relative safety.

Although plains zebras enjoy stable populations across much of their current habitat—even in unprotected areas—their numbers have been steadily declining. Competition with domestic animals for grazing land is the biggest threat to these zebras. And even though zebras are a protected species, poaching is rampant in many African countries, including Rwanda, Somalia, and South and North Sudan, where recent civil wars have made the protection of wildlife a low priority for unstable governments.

Much research on plains zebras is conducted during the great zebra migrations, when bands of zebras join together to follow the annual rainfall toward greener feeding grounds. The largest zebra migration occurs on

the Serengeti Plain of Tanzania and Kenya. Botswana, in southern Africa, is the location of the Makgadikgadi zebra migration, the second-largest migration. This annual event has been the subject of much recent research, including National Geographic's television documentary series *Great Migrations* (2010).

Every year, as the rainy season approaches, tens of thousands of zebras, wildebeest, gazelles, and many other animals travel hundreds of miles from the Okavango Delta to the Makgadikgadi Pan to feed on rain-soaked vegetation. In 1958, a fence to separate wildlife from

About 1.5 million wildebeest and 300,000 zebras and antelope make the annual 1,800-mile (2,897 km) trek across the Serengeti.

Zebras may be communal in the wild, but their territorial nature prevents their being housed with other hoofed animals in zoos.

domestic livestock was built across Botswana. The 800-mile-long (1,287 km) fence—as well as 14 other fences in Botswana and Namibia—block thousands of wild animals from reaching water sources, and hundreds of thousands of large mammals die of thirst each year. Another fence to keep wildlife from competing with cattle for water along the Boteti River in Botswana was proposed in 2001 and took three years to be built.

British scientists James Bradley and Chris Brooks of the University of Bristol began studying zebra migrations to learn about the ecological impact of fencing practices. They used GPS devices on collars to track zebra movements and also studied the quantity and quality of grasses that the animals typically fed on during their migration. When the Boteti River fence was completed in 2004, Bradley and Brooks launched the first large-scale study devoted to learning about the fence's effects on migrating herds. In collecting data on changes in migration patterns and differences in grasses available to the zebras, the researchers hope to formulate long-term strategies for conservation of zebras in a changing world.

Continued interest in the welfare of zebras will be needed from conservationists, citizens, and governments all across Africa, if the remaining zebra herds are to be adequately protected and managed. As a central link in the African ecosystem, zebras are vital to the health of their neighboring creatures, from the largest predators to the smallest scavengers. Without our help, zebras could disappear from the once boundless African wilderness forever.

Since foals need to drink at more regular intervals than adults, groups of zebras with young stay close to water.

People have interbred zebras with horses or donkeys, but offspring are rare, and those born, called zebroids, are always sterile.

ANIMAL TALE:
HOW THE ZEBRA LOST ITS HORNS

The zebra is part of the artwork, celebrations, and storytelling of numerous cultures throughout Central Africa. This myth from Botswana explains why the zebra does not have horns today, while many other African animals feature them.

Long ago, Zebra was a brilliant white animal with long, dark horns that stood straight upward like warrior spears. Zebra was proud of his appearance, and when he met other animals at the watering hole, he often boasted about his fine white coat and stunning horns.

One day, Oryx arrived at the watering hole. This animal was unlike any other in the area. He had a saggy coat of white and black stripes; long, striped legs; and a long, black face with a white mask. Many of the animals made fun of Oryx's odd appearance, including Zebra.

"You look like you are wearing baggy pajamas," said Zebra.

This made Oryx sad. He admired Zebra's brilliant white coat and, especially, his long horns. "How I wish I could have your horns," he said to Zebra.

Zebra laughed. "You are far too strange-looking to add such ornaments to your head."

"Perhaps you would let me try them on," said Oryx, "just to see how they look."

This made Zebra laugh harder. All the other animals at the watering hole—Thomson's Gazelle, Wildebeest, Rhinoceros, and Lion—began to laugh as well. "Let him try," said Wildebeest, who was surely more odd-looking than Oryx but did not let the fact bother him.

Zebra thought how entertaining it would be to make fun of Oryx with horns on his head, so he agreed.

"But only for a little while," he said to Oryx as he reached up to his head and unfastened his horns.

Oryx took the horns and carefully fastened them to the top of his own head. Leaning over the watering hole, Oryx looked at his reflection and smiled broadly, pleased with his new appearance. "I look quite fine, indeed," he said.

"You look ridiculous!" shouted Wildebeest.

Oryx, feeling hurt by this remark, said to Zebra, "I believe I'll just keep these horns, if you don't mind." And with that, he ran away as fast as he could from the watering hole.

Zebra was angry at this betrayal and chased after Oryx. Catching up, he leaped on Oryx's back and reached for the horns, but Oryx's baggy coat slipped off, and Zebra tumbled to the ground, tangled in Oryx's striped coat.

Oryx looked over his shoulder, feeling a bit guilty, but when he heard the curses that Zebra shouted at him, he decided to keep running. This is why Oryx now wears only his brown underclothes. He still has his striped legs and his white-masked face, but now he wears horns as straight and as sharp as spears.

Feeling sorry for himself, Zebra trudged back to the watering hole, wrapped tightly in Oryx's striped coat. "Help me get this off," he said to Wildebeest.

"Oh no," Wildebeest replied. "I think it suits you."

"What?" Zebra shouted.

"You should not have been so boastful of your beautiful coat and long horns," replied Wildebeest. "Now you have lost both because you wanted to mock Oryx. You should have to live in that striped coat forever."

And so Zebra does.

GLOSSARY

adapted – changed to improve its chances of survival in its environment

camouflage – the ability to hide, due to coloring or markings that blend in with a given environment

captive-reared – raised in a place from which escape is not possible

coat of arms – the official symbol of a family, state, nation, or other group

domesticated – tamed to be kept as a pet or used as a work animal

ecosystem – a community of organisms that live together in an environment

evaporates – changes from liquid to invisible vapor, or gas

evolved – gradually developed into a new form

extinction – the act or process of becoming extinct; coming to an end or dying out

genetic – relating to genes, the basic physical units of heredity

gestation – the period of time it takes a baby to develop inside its mother's womb

Global Positioning System – a system of satellites, computers, and other electronic devices that work together to determine the location of objects or living things that carry a trackable device

migration – a seasonal journey from one place to another and then back again

parasites – animals or plants that live on or inside another living thing (called a host) while giving nothing back to the host; some parasites cause disease or even death

pigment – a material or substance present in the tissues of animals or plants that gives them their natural coloring

poaching – hunting protected species of wild animals, even though doing so is against the law

regalia – the ceremonial clothing of a particular group, tribe, or culture

sterile – incapable of producing offspring

totem – an object, animal, or plant respected as a symbol of a tribe and often used in ceremonies and rituals

zoologists – people who study animals and their lives

SELECTED BIBLIOGRAPHY

African Wildlife Foundation. "Grevy's Zebra Conservation." http://www.awf.org/section/wildlife/zebras.

Kostyal, Karen M. *Great Migrations*. New York: National Geographic Society, 2010.

Makgadikgadi Zebra Migration. "Homepage." http://www.zebramigration.org.

Masson, Jeffrey Moussaieff. *Altruistic Armadillos, Zenlike Zebras: Understanding the World's Most Intriguing Animals.* New York: Skyhorse Publishing, 2009.

San Diego Zoo. "Animal Bytes: Zebra." http://www.sandiegozoo.org/animalbytes/t-zebra.html.

Skinner, J. D., and Christian T. Chimimba. *The Mammals of the Southern African Subregion.* Cambridge: Cambridge University Press, 2005.

While zebras cannot run as fast as horses, they have much greater stamina and can run at top speed for miles.

INDEX